Amazing Animals
Baboons

Please visit our Web site, www.garethstevens.com. For a free color catalog of all our high-quality books, call toll free 1-800-542-2595 or fax 1-877-542-2596.

Library of Congress Cataloging-in-Publication Data

Wilsdon, Christina.
  Baboons / Christina Wilsdon.
    p. cm. — (Amazing animals)
  Includes index.
  ISBN 978-1-4339-4005-7 (pbk.)
  ISBN 978-1-4339-4006-4 (6-pack)
  ISBN 978-1-4339-4004-0 (library binding)
  1. Baboons—Juvenile literature. I. Title.
  QL737.P93W553 2011
  599.8′65—dc22
                                        2010000489

This edition first published in 2011 by
Gareth Stevens Publishing
111 East 14th Street, Suite 349
New York, NY 10003

This edition copyright © 2011 Gareth Stevens Publishing.
Original edition copyright © 2006 by Readers' Digest Young Families.

Editor: Greg Roza
Designer: Christopher Logan

Photo credits: Cover, back cover, pp. 1, 3, 8–9 (all), 18–19, 24–25, 38–39, 42–43, 44–45 Shutterstock.com; pp. 4–5, 22–23 © Dynamic Graphics, Inc.;
pp. 6–7, 12–13, 20–21 © Jupiter Images; pp. 10–11 © Image Source; pp. 14–15 © Dreamstime.com/Steve Meyfroidt; pp. 16–17 © Brand X Pictures;
pp. 26–27 PhotoDisc Green/Getty Images; pp. 28–29, 36–37 © Dreamstime.com/Jurie Maree; p. 29 (inset) © iStockphoto.com/Davina Graham;
pp. 30–31 © Image 100 Ltd.; pp. 32–33 © Dreamstime.com/Johannes G. Swanepoel; p. 33 (inset) © Dreamstime.com/Jeff Shultes;
pp. 34–35 courtesy U.S. Fish & Wildlife Service; p. 46 Wikimedia Commons.

Printed in the United States of America

CPSIA compliance information: Batch #CS10GS: For further information contact Gareth Stevens, New York, New York at 1-800-542-2595.

Amazing Animals
Baboons

By Christina Wilsdon

Gareth Stevens
Publishing

Contents

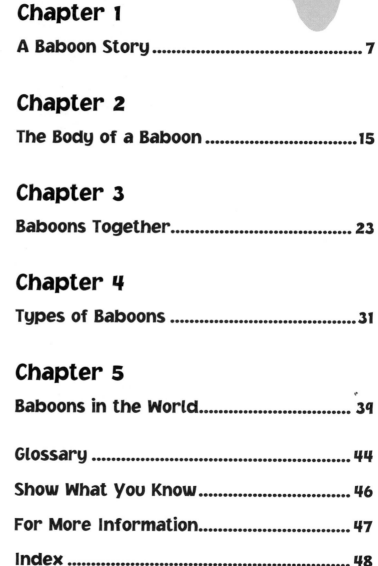

Chapter 1

Chapter 1
A Baboon Story

Baby Baboons

A baby baboon weighs only about 2 pounds (1 kg) when it is born. It has black fur and pink skin. When it is 6 months old, it will start to lose its black baby fur and grow the same color fur as an adult baboon.

Baby Baboon clutched his mother's fur with his hands and feet. Clinging to Mama Baboon's belly was a great way to get around—even if it was upside down! Baby Baboon was just a few days old, so he was still too little and weak to walk by himself. Hanging onto Mama Baboon was enough hard work!

Mama Baboon took good care of her baby. She cuddled him close so he could drink her milk. She combed his black baby fur with her fingers and picked off any bugs she found. At night, she held him tight as she slept on a branch in a tree.

All the baboons in the **troop** were very interested in Baby Baboon. Many of these baboons were aunts and cousins and sisters. Mama Baboon let the other baboons touch her baby. Sometimes she let them hold him and **groom** him.

Holding On!

For the first few months of its life, a baby baboon spends most of the time clinging to its mother's belly. It even travels that way!

One day Baby Baboon slowly let go of his mother's fur. He was 2 weeks old and ready for some adventure! First he let his feet drop to the ground. He hung on with his hands for a few seconds longer. Then he spread his fingers. *Thump!* He sat down on the ground with a surprised look on his face.

Mama Baboon watched carefully as Baby Baboon began to explore. He did not stray too far. He just explored the area around her feet. Then he jumped back into her arms and snuggled up for a nap.

By the time he was 3 weeks old, Baby Baboon was spending more time on the ground. He sat by Mama Baboon's side and watched her find food. He sampled what she ate. He even tried to groom her fur with his little hands.

Sometimes Baby Baboon tried to wander away from his mother. But Mama Baboon never let him go too far. As soon as he moved out of reach, she snatched him up. She knew that leopards, hyenas, and other **predators** were always ready to grab a baby baboon. As Baby Baboon got older, Mama Baboon let him wander a little farther away. He began playing with other baby baboons.

I Don't Want to Grow Up

A baby baboon's childhood lasts about 3 years. By then, it has learned how to live in a group. A female stays with the same troop all her life. A male finds a new troop when he is about 7 years old.

Ride 'em, Baboon!

When it is about 10 weeks old, a baby baboon starts to ride on its mother's back. At first, it lies on her back. But as it gets older, it will sit up like a horseback rider. Mom raises her tail so the baby can lean on it.

Baby Baboon rolled and **wrestled** with other baby baboons. Sometimes the play got rough. Then Baby Baboon ran to Mama Baboon until he felt brave enough to play again. Baby Baboon also spent time with grown-up baboons—especially his big sister. She did not have a baby of her own yet. She liked to pick up Baby Baboon and groom him all over.

One day Baby Baboon wandered a bit too far from the troop. Suddenly, an eagle dove at him! He dashed back to the safety of Mama Baboon's arms. The rest of the troop jumped up and down and shouted "Wahoo!" at the eagle.

As Baby Baboon grows, he will drink less of his mother's milk. Mama Baboon will even push him away when he tries to nurse. By the time Baby Baboon is 1 year old, he will gather almost all his own food. When he is 7 or 8 years old, he will leave to find a new troop to join. Someday he may even become the leader.

Chapter 2
The Body of a Baboon

A male baboon can weigh up to 90 pounds (40 kg). All male baboons are about twice as big as female baboons.

Getting Around

A baboon is a **species** of monkey. It can climb trees easily, but it spends most of its time on the ground. A baboon may walk 2 miles (3.2 km) or more in 1 day looking for food.

When a baboon walks, it places the soles of its feet and the palms of its hands flat on the ground. This is different from the way great apes such as chimpanzees and gorillas walk. These animals curl up their fingers and walk on their knuckles, not on their palms.

The Baboon's Hands and Feet

Like other monkeys, a baboon has hands and feet that are good for holding onto things. It has four long fingers and a thumb on each hand, just like a human. A baboon can peel away the tough skin of a fruit or use its flat nails to pick up tiny seeds. Some baboons can even untie knots!

Each foot has four long toes and a thumblike fifth toe that helps in climbing trees. A baboon can even hold objects with its feet. This is especially useful at night, when it sleeps sitting up in a tree—it uses its feet to hold on to the branch.

Common Senses

A baboon's eyes sit just above its long **muzzle**, and they face forward. This helps the baboon judge how far away things are and see close objects clearly. A baboon can see in color, which helps it find fresh fruit and young leaves to eat. A baboon also has excellent hearing.

A baboon's sense of smell is not as sensitive as that of many other animals. So baboons have learned to watch other animals for clues of danger. A herd of grazing **impala** that suddenly stops and looks nervous may have picked up the scent of a leopard!

Making Faces

A baboon uses its face to **communicate** with other baboons. An annoyed baboon shows off the pale color of its eyelids by raising its eyebrows and staring. An angry baboon shows its teeth. A baboon often lets others know it is friendly by making a "kissy face" and smacking its lips.

Not Your Usual Monkey Face

A baboon is sometimes called a "dog-faced monkey" because of its long muzzle. Most monkeys have flat faces.

This baboon makes a special face that means "Let's play!" by opening its mouth wide and covering its teeth with its lips.

When male baboons show off their sharp fangs, it may end up in a real fight—especially if they both like the same female!

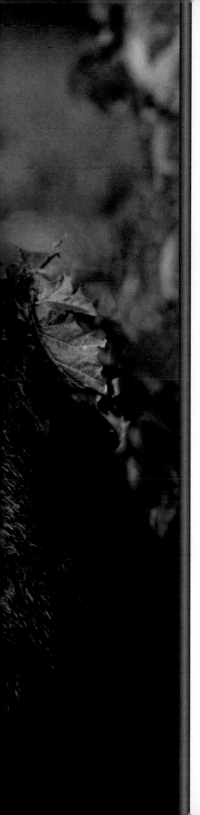

A Baboon's Bite

A baboon has 32 teeth—just like an adult human. The biggest teeth are the sharp fangs called **canines**. A male's canines are much bigger than the female's. They can be up to 2.5 inches (6.4 cm) long!

Males sometimes use their fangs to fight over females. The **dominant** male, usually the most important one in the troop, often opens his mouth in a huge fake yawn just to show off his fangs. This is meant to warn other males that might want to challenge him. Big fangs also help males defend their troops against predators.

Backseat Padding

Many baboons sleep sitting on tree branches. This may sound uncomfortable, but a baboon has a built-in "pillow" on its backside! This seat is not soft. It is formed by a pair of rough, thick pads. The pads have very few nerves in them, which means the baboon's bottom doesn't feel a thing when it sits on a hard branch or rough ledge.

Chapter 3
Baboons Together

Living in a troop helps baboons survive. Many pairs of eyes and ears are on the alert for danger.

Safety in Numbers

Life in the grasslands is a challenge for baboons. Hungry leopards, lions, hyenas, and jackals are always looking for **prey**. A baboon alone is a baboon in danger! That is why baboons live in troops. A typical troop may contain 30 to 50 baboons. If a predator attacks, it will be met by many angry baboons—including a few sharp-fanged males!

A baboon in a troop also learns from the other troop members. Older baboons know where to find food, and they know the trails and other facts about their **habitat**.

Who's the Boss?

Male and female baboons play different roles in a troop. Females stay with the same troop throughout their lives. Each female has a certain **rank** in the troop. A female with a high rank can boss around females of lower rank. A low-ranking female will move if a high-ranking female wants to sit in her spot!

A young male can boss around weaker males. But when a male grows up, he must leave his troop. He is on his own until he joins a new troop. Males becomes troop leaders by fighting other males. A leader may keep his rank for as little as a month, but some males keep their top rank for many years.

Baboon Babies

A baby baboon is helpless at first. It needs constant care from its mother. She will take care of it until it is about 1 year old. After that, she will no longer carry it or let it nurse, but she will still groom it. She will also defend it when it gets into quarrels with other baboons.

Friends Forever

Female baboons who are related share a strong bond. Mothers, daughters, sisters, aunts, and cousins groom each other. They stick up for each other, too. If a female gets into a fight with another female, her female relatives help her out by ganging up on the troublemaker. A baby baboon can also count on these relatives for help. If the baby is female, she is born with her mother's rank.

Sometimes a low-ranking baboon can change her rank. As older females die, a high-ranking female may not have enough relatives around to help her in quarrels. A low-ranking female and her family can challenge her and take her place in the troop.

Baboons are fascinated by baby baboons. A female's mother, sisters, aunts, and nieces all want to touch and groom her baby.

Baboons spend lots of time grooming each other. They run their fingers through each other's fur, picking out dirt and insects.

A Monkey's Uncle

A female baboon often has a male friend in addition to her female buddies. He is usually a low-ranking male who has quietly formed a friendship with her. Sometimes he is new to the troop. Making friends with the females helps him join the troop.

A male who is friends with a female sits near her. The two baboons groom each other. The male is gentle and patient with the female's baby. He plays with the baby and lets it climb all over him. He will even share his food. He protects the little one from predators and defends it in fights.

Sometimes a male baboon will scoop up the baby if he feels threatened by another male. Carrying a baby baboon will usually stop the other male from attacking him.

What's on the Menu?

Baboons are **omnivores**, which means they eat both plants and meat. They are not picky eaters. They like grasses, fruit, and insects. Sometimes they enjoy rabbits, lizards, baby antelope, and birds.

Types of Baboons

A male Guinea baboon, like this one, is about 27 inches (69 cm) long and weighs about 50 pounds (23 kg) when fully grown.

Five of a Kind

Four baboon species live in Africa's grasslands, which are called **savannas**. They are called savanna baboons. A fifth species lives in the northeast part of Africa and the Arabian peninsula.

The smallest baboon is a savanna species called the Guinea baboon. A Guinea baboon's fur is red-brown, and the sitting pads on its rear end are pink. Guinea baboons live in the grasslands and woodlands of only a few countries in western Africa.

The largest baboon, called the chacma baboon, is also a savanna species. An adult male can be about 32 inches (81 cm)

long and weigh about 70 pounds (32 kg). An especially big male may weigh up to 90 pounds (41 kg). Chacma baboons live in the grasslands and woodlands of southern Africa. Most have black-brown fur on their backs, with lighter fur on their bellies.

Green Ones

Olive baboons are named after the color of their fur, which is gray or brown mixed with olive green. Their faces, ears, and sitting pads are dark gray or black. Males have long manes that flow from the tops of their heads to their shoulders.

Olive baboons are found in many countries across Africa. They live in savannas, in woodlands, and in forests near rivers. Many scientists have studied olive baboons over the past 50 years. Much of what we know about baboons comes from these studies.

Yellow Ones

Yellow baboons are also named for their fur color, which is yellow-brown. A yellow baboon's face is black with some white fur around the muzzle. Most baby yellow baboons have black fur, although they are born with red or white fur in some parts of Africa.

Yellow baboons are found in many countries across the middle of Africa. They live in grasslands and woodlands. In some places, they share their habitat with other baboon species.

A troop of olive baboons may have as few as 15 or as many as 150 members. The troop has a few adult males, like this one, and many females and young baboons.

Although many savanna baboons live in dry places, the hamadryas baboon is able to survive in habitats that are much drier—almost as dry as deserts.

Silver Ones

Hamadryas (ha-muh-DRY-uhs) baboons live in the dry lands of northeastern Africa and in Saudi Arabia and Yemen. They have pink or red sitting pads. Males have silvery gray fur that grows long over their shoulders, forming a heavy cape. Females have gray-brown fur. Hamadryas baboons seem to know where to find pools of water—and where to dig for water if the pools run dry.

A Different Baboon Band

Hamadryas baboons live in small groups that are very different from savanna baboon troops. A hamadryas baboon group is called a one-male unit. Scientists call this "**OMU**" for short. An OMU is made up of one male, some females, and all their young. The male protects and leads the group.

All the females in the OMU groom and obey the leader. They bond more closely with the leader than with each other. Anyone who disobeys him risks a sharp bite to the neck!

At night, a number of OMUs come together to form one big troop. They gather at cliffs and sleep on ledges. In the morning, the OMUs separate to look for food.

Chapter 5
Baboons in the World

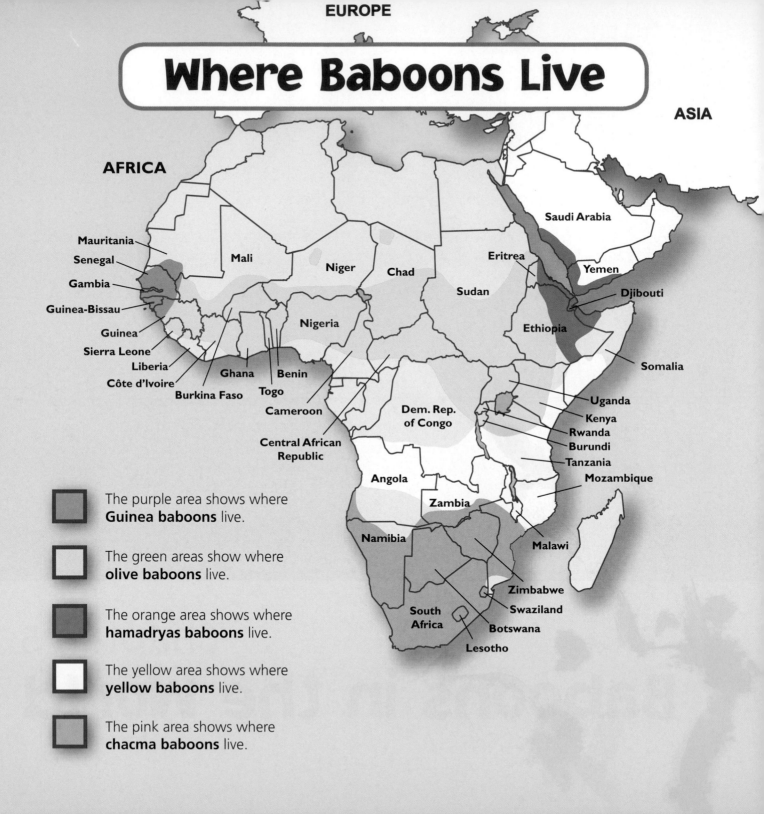

Where Baboons Live

EUROPE

ASIA

AFRICA

Mauritania
Senegal
Gambia
Guinea-Bissau
Guinea
Sierra Leone
Liberia
Côte d'Ivoire
Ghana
Burkina Faso
Togo
Benin
Cameroon
Central African
Republic

Mali
Niger
Chad
Nigeria

Saudi Arabia
Eritrea
Sudan
Yemen
Djibouti
Ethiopia
Somalia

Dem. Rep.
of Congo

Uganda
Kenya
Rwanda
Burundi
Tanzania
Mozambique

Angola
Zambia

Namibia

Malawi

Zimbabwe
Swaziland
Botswana
Lesotho

South
Africa

The purple area shows where **Guinea baboons** live.

The green areas show where **olive baboons** live.

The orange area shows where **hamadryas baboons** live.

The yellow area shows where **yellow baboons** live.

The pink area shows where **chacma baboons** live.

Baboons in History

Ancient Egyptians believed the hamadryas baboon was sacred. They thought the baboon was a living form of Thot, the Egyptian god of writing. Some baboons were kept in temples. They were even made into mummies after they died.

Archaeologists have found statues of baboons in Egyptian temples. Baboons appear in paintings on walls, too. The paintings show baboons performing chores such as sweeping and picking fruit. Did baboons really do these chores? Nobody knows for sure.

Studying Baboons

Today, scientists study baboons to learn more about diseases and the medicines that might cure them. Scientists also study baboon behavior. It was once believed baboons were fierce animals that fought all the time. But studies have shown that this is not so. Scientists learned that female baboons control much of the behavior in a troop. Some researchers even discovered a troop of peaceful baboons that turned away bossy males!

The Future of Baboons

Baboons are very adaptable. This means they are able to live in different kinds of habitats. They eat many different kinds of food, which helps them adapt to changes in their environment. Being adaptable has also helped baboons survive in places where humans have changed their habitats.

However, being adaptable sometimes puts baboons in conflict with humans. As Africa's human population grows, more land is used for farming. Baboons see the crops as a good food source. Many baboons are killed by farmers trying to protect their crops. In some parts of South Africa, baboons wander through towns and even break into homes.

People are working to make peace among farmers, villagers, and baboons. Sometimes baboon troops are caught and moved away from farmland to wildlife preserves. Villagers are taught to store trash so it does not attract baboons.

Fast Facts About Olive Baboons

Scientific name	*Papio anubis*
Class	Mammalia
Order	Primates
Size	Up to 29 inches (74 cm) long, not including tail
Weight	Male—up to 80 pounds (36 kg) Female—up to 33 pounds (15 kg)
Life span	25 years in the wild 30 to 40 years in captivity
Habitat	Savanna and open woodlands

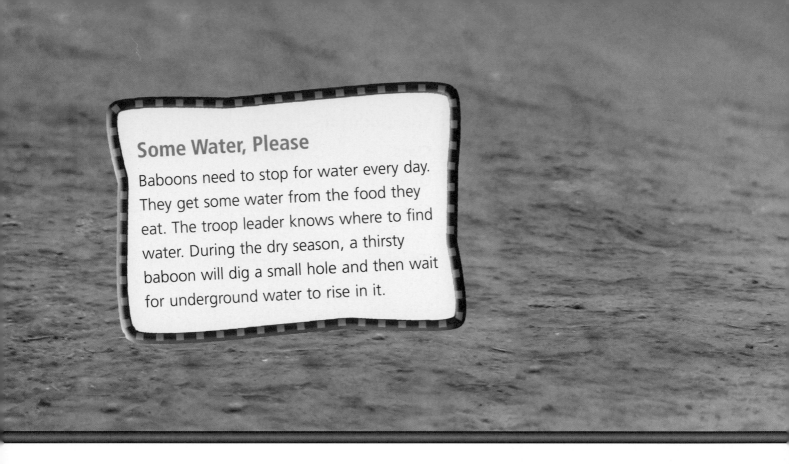

Some Water, Please

Baboons need to stop for water every day. They get some water from the food they eat. The troop leader knows where to find water. During the dry season, a thirsty baboon will dig a small hole and then wait for underground water to rise in it.

Glossary

archaeologist—someone who studies the remains of past civilizations

canines—long, sharp teeth that are sometimes called fangs

communicate—to share knowledge or information

dominant—the most powerful or strongest

groom—to clean the fur, feathers, or skin

habitat—the natural environment where an animal or plant lives

impala—an animal with curved horns that is similar to a deer

muzzle—the snout of an animal, consisting of the jaws and nose

omnivore—an animal that eats both plants and meat

OMU—a one-male unit, made up of one male baboon, some females, and all their children

predator—an animal that hunts and eats other animals to survive

prey—animals that are hunted by other animals for food

rank—a baboon's position in a troop

savanna—a grassland with scattered patches of trees

species—a group of living things that are the same

troop—a group of baboons that live together

wrestle—to try to push or hold another person down

Baboons: Show What You Know

How much have you learned about baboons? Grab a piece of paper and a pencil and write your answers down.

1. About how much does a baby baboon weigh at birth?

2. At what age does a male baboon leave his troop to join a new one?

3. Which of a baboon's senses is not as sensitive as that of many other animals?

4. How do baboons let others know they are being friendly?

5. How many teeth does an adult baboon have?

6. How many baboons are in a typical troop?

7. What is the largest baboon species?

8. Much of what we know about baboons comes from the study of which baboon species?

9. What does "OMU" stand for?

10. Which ancient culture believed hamadryas baboons were sacred?

1. 2 pounds (1 kg) 2. 7 or 8 years 3. Smell 4. By making "kissy faces" and smacking their lips 5. 32 6. 30 to 50 baboons 7. The chacma baboon 8. The olive baboon 9. One-male unit 10. Egyptian

For More Information

Books

Lockwood, Sophie. *Baboons*. Chanhassen, MN: Child's World, 2006.
Stewart, Melissa. *Baboons*. Minneapolis, MN: Lerner Publications, 2007.

Web Sites

Baboon
www.awf.org/content/wildlife/detail/baboon
Read about baboons and find out how you can help protect them and their habitats.

Baboon
animals.nationalgeographic.com/animals/mammals/baboon.html
Learn all about baboons and see pictures of them in their natural habitats.

Index